SMALL BUSINESS:

A Step By Step Primer

Published by William La Rue, Jr.

First Printing, 2014

ISBN 978-0-692-39106-8

Cover and Book Designs by William La Rue, Jr.

Contents:

STEP I: STRUCTURE

If you have not already selected and filed for your business structure, now is the time to accomplish this.

You may choose to operate as a Sole Proprietorship (dba); a Limited Liability Company (LLC); a C-Corporation (C-Corp); an S-Corporation (S-Corp); or a Partnership. To help you decide which is right for you, I would suggest going to your local Small Business Administration (SBA) office to discuss the options and follow that visit up with discussions with your attorney/accountant.

Whatever structure you select will have legal and tax implications so be sure and seek professional advice.

STEP II: THE PLAN

By selecting this text you have shown you are committed to the task of starting a business or expanding /understanding your current business. Now is the time to put your ideas into a formalized plan.....THE BUSINESS PLAN.

You must first understand that a successful business plan is an ongoing "living" document. Do not allow it to die by tucking it away in a desk drawer somewhere. Keep it handy always because as your business evolves, its characteristics will change and thus the business plan will require modifications in order to keep you moving forward successfully.

Not only are you developing a business plan for you to operate around but you are also going to use it as a very effective tool to tell significant others i.e., financing sources, your "story" of:

- Where you are
- Where you desire to go
- How you plan on getting there

The following is an Outline for an effective Business Plan and what it should contain. There is no need to write a lengthy novel regarding your plan but you do need to _be specific_ enough to allow the reader to be able to answer all the questions that may arise for them in their understanding of your business.

To get started, one good method of developing the content of the plan is to study over and understand the various sections of the plan and then each day as you think about it, jot down your thoughts _as they happen_, on sticky notes, and place those notes on a large paper on a wall under Outline section titles.

BUSINESS PLAN GUIDELINES:

Remember: Keep it simple yet detailed. A few sentences/a couple of paragraphs under each section/subsection.

1. **Title Page:** This is the cover sheet to the Plan
   - Business name
   - Business address
   - Business telephone number
   - Owner's name(s)

2. **Business Concept:**
   - What does your business do? (1 to 2 sentences)
   - To whom will you market your services / products? (2 sentences tops)
   - Why is your business service/product in demand? (3 to 4 sentences)
   - Who is your competition? (2 sentences tops)
   - Why are you more effective than the competition? (2-3 sentences)

3. **Marketing Plan:**
   - Describe your potential customers: (Give a few examples and include, ages, sex, location). In other words who is in need of your services/products? How do you plan to reach them?
   - What sets your abilities apart from anyone else attempting to provide the same service/product? (3 to 4 sentences)
   - Describe any special surroundings or environment that might be required for you to offer your services/products. In other words do you need special spaces in which to conduct your business or are you just out in the field? LOCATION???
   - Pricing for Services/Products: What will you charge for your services/products? How would your pricing compare with existing services/products offered by others?

4. **Management / Operations:**
   - Are there any licenses required by you in order to offer your services/products?
   - Do you need the advice of any legal services to operate without risk? Who?
   - Do you need any written "hold harmless" agreements / waivers to be signed by your clients?
   - Will you need to hire employees? If so, how many, what type, what skills?
   - Availability of required labor market?

5. **Financial Plan:** (Be specific here and provide underlying assumptions)
   - How much money is needed to begin operations?

- What will these funds be used for?

6. **Strategic Plan:**
   - Where do you want your business to go in the future (Revenues; locations; # of employees; geographic area served, etc.)? Time needed?
   - How do you grow your business to reach future goals?

One important note regarding your future submission of this Business Plan to any financing source/investors:

The following documents should accompany this Business Plan to complete any loan request / investor's package:

- Existing business balance sheets and income statements for 3 years
- Interim (current) year to date balance sheet and income statement
- Cash Flow Statement
- Three (3) years of business tax returns including Schedules & K-1s
- Personal financial statement
- Three (3) years of personal tax returns
- Business financial projections for 3 years
- Break even analysis
- Accounts Receivable aging report
- List of debts schedule showing creditor's name; loan date; original loan amount; current balance; monthly payment amount; interest rate; collateral pledged

Most of the above forms are explained/described in the STEPS that follow.

STEP III: BUSINESS JARGON

Your accountant and any finance related sources you may require will use a specialized vocabulary to define your business operations. It is important that you understand these various terms and what they describe. You will see these terms used over and over again in financial statements, tax returns, and any financial analysis. Here is a list and description of the most common:

Balance Sheet:

A report of the Assets, Liabilities, Equity (Capital) or Net Worth of the subject of the report. The Assets are on the left half of the report and the Liabilities and Equity or Net Worth appear on the right half. The total of the left side (Assets) will equal the total of the Liabilities plus Equity, or Net Worth, on the right side, hence a "balance sheet".

Assets – Liabilities = Equity or Net Worth &

Assets = Liabilities + Equity or Net Worth.

Assets

Everything that is owned by the subject (business or individual) of the balance sheet. *Keep in mind this list includes both encumbered and unencumbered (debt free) assets.*

Short term assets ("Current Assets"): Those that are fairly liquid and can be converted to cash or used up in the operation of the business over a short period of time, less than 12 months. Examples are cash itself, listed stocks (marketable securities), inventory (raw materials, work in process, and finished goods), trade accounts receivable (amounts due from customers for merchandise or services purchased on an open account), prepaid expenses, and cash value life insurance.

Long term assets ("Fixed Assets"): Those not so quickly converted to cash such as real estate, vehicles, equipment, etc. and having a useful life of over 12 months. Their values are reduced on a business balance sheet over time by the amount these assets have been *depreciated* by accounting rules. Your accountant will be calculating and tracking the depreciation of these business assets. Ask your accountant how the depreciation is calculated (over the depreciable life of those assets) and used as a non-cash expense each year to reduce your tax burden.

Liabilities

Everything that is <u>owed</u> by the subject (debts of the business or individual) of the balance sheet.

Short term liabilities: Those debts that are payable in 12 months or less such as trade accounts payable [owed to a creditor (typically a vendor) for goods or services on an open account]; current maturities of long term debt (that portion of a long term loan that is scheduled to be paid back during a 12 month period); and most revolving lines of credit.

Long term liabilities: That portion of debt obligations payable over a period longer than 12 months such as a real estate mortgage or equipment term loans. <u>Remember</u>: The short term portion has already been subtracted from the debt balance and reported as "current maturities of long term debt". Therefore term debt has 2 components, the current maturities or short term portion and the long term portion.

Owner's Equity ("Capital"): On a business balance sheet your accountant will divide the equity in the business into two categories, namely *common stock* and *retained earnings*.

Here is a sample of the format for a typical Business Balance Sheet:

ASSETS:
Cash..................... $_____
Inventory...............$_____
Accounts Receivable...$_____
Marketable Securities $_____
Prepaid Expenses ...$_____
Total Current Assets...$_____

Long Term Assets.....
Land.......................$_____
Buildings.................$_____
Equipment...............$_____
Less Accum. Deprec.$_(_____)
Total Long Term Assets.$_____

Total Assets.................$_____

LIABILITIES:
Current Mat. LTD....$_____
Accounts payable...$_____
Accrued Salary........$_____
Taxes Payable.........$_____
Accrued Expenses...$_____
Total Current Liabilities..$_____

Long Term Liabilities.....
Term debt, LT portion.$_____
Other.........................$_____
Total L.T. Liabilities......$_____
Total Liabilities............$_____

Owner's Equity............$_____
Total Liabilities and
Owner's Equity.............$_____

Income Statement:

This is also referred to as a Profit and Loss Statement or "P & L". This report is a summary of the revenues, costs, and expenses for a business over a *specified period of time*.

Revenues (Gross Sales).
Your amount charged during this specific period for your goods or services.

Net Sales.
The Gross Sales minus any returns and allowances (discounts).

Cost of Goods Sold.
The cost of buying raw materials to produce the finished goods that were sold and the cost of your inventory to include the cost to bring it to you.

Gross profit.
Net Sales less the Cost of Goods Sold. This is your profit prior to deducting operating expenses.

G & A Expenses (operating expenses).
The **G**eneral and **A**dministrative expenses of operating your business to include such things as rent, salaries, payroll taxes, legal and accounting expense, interest paid, depreciation taken, insurances, repairs and maintenance, utilities and phones, property taxes, marketing/advertising, travel & entertainment. These expenses can be either "fixed" or "variable".

Net Income (profit).
The pre-tax profit after all expenses of operation are paid. Of course, *if expenses outweigh revenues there is a **net loss** rather than net income.*

"EBITDA".
A term related to the **E**arnings of the business **B**efore the expenses of **I**nterest, **T**axes, **D**epreciation and **A**mortization. Sometimes called "operating cash flow" however this term is mainly used in large

companies that have a large amount of assets and a large amount of debt to service interest on. "Amortization" refers to the spreading out of the cost of an *intangible* asset (such as a patent) over the useful life of that intangible asset where "Depreciation" is a spreading out of the cost of a *tangible* asset such as machinery or real estate over its useful life.

Below is a sample of a business income statement:

INCOME STATEMENT (P&L)

Gross Sales	
Less: Ret. & Allow.	
Net Sales............................	
Cost of Goods	
GROSS PROFIT...........................	

G & A Expenses

Salary Expense	
Rent	
Payroll taxes	
Travel & Enter.	
Prof. & Acctg	
Depreciation	
Insurance	
Interest	
Rep & Maint.	
Util. & Phone	
Office Supplies	
Property taxes	
Marketing	
Other Expense	

Total G&A Expenses....................

Net Income................................
Income Taxes.............................
Net Income after tax......................

Business Cash Flow Statement:

A statement representing _sources_ of cash coming in to the business ("inflow") as well as _sources_ of cash going out of the business ("outflow") during a specified period of time.

Changes that take place in the reported value of various balance sheet items from the beginning of a specified period to the end of that specified period have either a positive or negative effect on cash flow.

For example:

Items that create cash inflow:

- Sales / revenues and "other cash receipts"
- Inventory decreases
- Accounts payable increases
- Accounts receivable decreases
- Incoming loan proceeds

Items that create cash outflow:

- Inventory increases
- Accounts payable decreases
- Accounts receivable increases
- Cost of Goods
- Operating expenses
- Salary expenses
- Income taxes
- Payments to loan principal
- Payments of loan interest
- Capital expenditures (buying "things" for use in the business)
- Owner's draws

The following is a sample of a typical Cash Flow Statement:

CASH FLOW STATEMENT

	Total
Cash Receipts	
Sales..	
Inventory Decreases (Increases)	
A/P Increases (Decreases)	
A/R Decreases (Increases)	
Total Cash Sales	
Financing Income	
Interest Income	
Loan Proceeds	
Other Cash Receipts	
Total Cash Receipts.................	
Cash Outflows	
Expenses	
Cost of Goods..........................	
Operating expenses...................	
Salary expenses........................	
Income taxes...........................	
Principal Loan Payments	
Interest Loan Payments...............	
Capital Expenditures	
Inventory Increases	
Owners Draw	
Total Cash Outflows..................	
Net Cash Flow........................	
Opening Cash Balance................	
Cash Receipts...........................	
Cash Outflows..........................	
Ending Cash Indicated..............	

STEP IV:
THE PERSONAL FINANCIAL STATEMENT

The personal financial statement is a snapshot of your personal financial health at a specific point in time.

It is important to you as an individual as it allows you to see at a glance what you have acquired as compared to what may be detracting from the value of what you have acquired.

It is important to your potential creditors / investors as it tells them your ability to provide a secondary source for repayment of debt or your ability to continue servicing operating expenses in the event the business should suffer a low point ("hiccup") in operational profitability.

The stronger your personal net worth and the more liquidity you show within that net worth; the more desirable you are as a credit / business risk.

Let's get started.

Be very detailed in completing the form and leave nothing unanswered. If you have nothing to report in a particular category or statement "Schedule" mark it as "NONE" so that the reader knows that you were aware of the section and truly had nothing to report. Don't leave them guessing.

Here are some important points to help you complete the personal financial statement ("PFS") in a professional manner:

- Each PFS should be addressed "To" a specific intended reader
- The PFS date, "as of" is important because if you use today's date then you are assuring the reader that the values given to the entries are in fact current to this date. If the figures are current as of your last calendar month end bank statement, then use that date.
- "Equity interests": If you are the sole owner of your business then you may report 100% of the Net Equity in that business that appears in the most recent Balance Sheet of the company. If you are a partner in a venture, report only your vested share in that entity's equity.
- "Accounts and Notes Receivable": If a family member or a related business concern owes you money, only enter the balance due you if you have a legally enforceable document that verifies the debt.
- "Mortgages and Land Contracts Receivable": If you sold real estate to another party and carried back a note payable to you then report it here.
- "Cash Value Life Insurance": **Do Not** enter here the <u>face value</u> of any life insurance policy you have unless that policy is paid up and you have the ability to borrow against that value. Only report cash value you have access to today. If in doubt, ask your insurance agent.
- "Other Assets: List here your vehicles, household goods (furniture & appliances to include electronics), stamp/coin collections, etc. at the value you believe it is worth today if you were to sell it.
- The liability side of the statement is pretty self-explanatory.
- Be sure and complete the "Schedules" related to the balance sheet entries as specified on the form.
- Answer all questions posed

- "Contingent Liabilities": These are obligations that you <u>may</u> <u>become responsible for</u> due to you being a party in an ongoing law suit; due to you cosigning a debt for others; agreements for back taxes owed, etc.
- Be sure to sign and date the last page of the form

THE FOLLOWING IS A SAMPLE OF A TYPICAL PERSONAL FINANCIAL STATEMENT FORM:

NOTE: <u>**If you will be seeking financing for your business, it is advised to obtain a blank personal financial statement form from your chosen finance source as most have their own preferred format.**</u>

PERSONAL FINANCIAL STATEMENT

CONFIDENTIAL

IMPORTANT: DIRECTIONS TO APPLICANT

To:

_____

Address:

_____

_____

_____

Personal Financial Statement as
of

_____

(DATE)

APPLICANT'S NAME(S):

_____

_____

HOME ADDRESS

_____

_____

_____

HOME PHONE

_____

Read directions before completing Financial Statement.

Please check appropriate box

☐ Individual credit—If relying on your own income and assets and not the

income and assets of a spouse or another person as a basis for

extension or repayment or credit, complete the Financial Statement below

only as it applies to you, individually. Do not provide any information

about a spouse or other person. Sign the Financial Statement.

☐ Joint Credit   If applying for joint credit or for individual credit relying

on income or assets of a spouse or another person

for extension and repayment of credit requested,

☐ Individual relying   complete the Financial Statement below. Include

upon income or   information about income, assets and liabilities of the

assets of spouse   spouse or other person. Both Applicant and Spouse

or other person.   or Co-Applicant sign this statement.

Please do not leave any questions unanswered. Use "no" or "none" where necessary.

Assets	In Even Dollars	Liabilities and Net Worth	In Even Dollars
Cash on hand and in Banks—See Schedule A	$	Notes Payable: This Bank—See Schedule A	$
U.S. Government Securities—See Schedule B		Notes Payable: Other Institutions—See Schedule A	
Listed Securities—See Schedule B			
Unlisted Securities—See Schedule B		Notes Payable—Relatives	
Other Equity Interests—See Schedule B		Notes Payable—Others	
Accounts and Notes Receivable		Accounts and Bills Due	
Real Estate Owned—See Schedule C		Unpaid Taxes	
Mortgages and Land Contracts Receivable— See Schedule D		Real Estate Mortgages Payable—See Schedule C or D	
Cash Value Life Insurance—See Schedule E		Land Contracts Payable—See Schedule C or D	
Other Assets: Itemize		Life Insurance Loans—See Schedule E	
		Other Liabilities: Itemize	
		TOTAL LIABILITIES	$
		NET WORTH	$
TOTAL ASSETS	$	TOTAL LIABILITIES AND NET WORTH	$

Sources of Income	In Even Dollars	General Information	
Salary	$	Employer	
Bonus and Commissions		Position or Profession	No. Years
Dividends		Employer's Address	
Real Estate Income			Phone No.
*Other Income: Itemize		Partner, officer or owner in any other venture? ☐ No ☐ Yes	
		If so, explain:	
TOTAL	$		

*Alimony, child support or separate maintenance payments need not be disclosed unless relied upon as a basis for extension of credit. If disclosed, payments received under ☐ court order ☐ written agreement ☐ oral understanding.

Are any assets pledged? ☐ No ☐ Yes Detail in Schedule A

Income taxes settled through (Date)

Contingent Liabilities	In Even Dollars	General Information (continued)
As endorser, co-maker or guarantor	$	Are you a defendant in any suits or legal action? ☐ No ☐ Yes
On leases		If so, explain:
Legal claims		Have you ever taken bankruptcy? ☐ No ☐ Yes
Provision for federal income taxes		If so, explain:
Other special debt, e.g., recourse or repurchase liability		Do you have a will? ☐ No ☐ Yes With whom?
		Do you have a trust? ☐ No ☐ Yes With whom?
TOTAL	$	Number of dependents _____ Ages _____

Schedule A: Banks, Brokers, Savings & Loan Association, Finance Companies or Credit Unions. List here the names of all the institutions at which you maintain a deposit account and/or where you have obtained loans.

Name of Institution	Name on Account	Balance on Deposit	High Credit	Amount Owing	Monthly Payment	Secured by What Assets
	TOTAL		**TOTAL**			

Schedule B: U.S. Governments, Stocks (Listed & Unlisted), Bonds (Gov't & Comm.), and Partnership Interests (General & Ltd.)

Number of	Indicate:			Pledged	
Shares, Face Value (Bonds), or % of Ownership	1. Agency or name of company issuing security or name of partnership 2. Type of investment or equity classification 3. Number of shares, bonds or % of ownership held 4. Basis of valuation*	In Name of	*Market Value	Yes (▣)	No (▣)
	TOTAL				

*If unlisted security or partnership interest, provide current financial statements to support basis for valuation.

Schedule C: Real Estate Owned (and related debt, if applicable)

Description of Property or Address	Title in Name Of	Date Acq.	Cost + Improvements	Present Mkt. Value	Mortgage or Land Contract Payable		
					Bal. Owing	Mo. Payt.	Holder
TOTAL							

Schedule D: Real Estate: Mortgages & Land Contracts Receivable (and related debt, if applicable)

Description of Property or Address	Title in Name Of	Date Acq.	Balance Receivable	Monthly Payment	Mortgage or Land Contract Payable		
					Bal. Owing	Mo. Payt.	Holder
TOTAL							

Schedule E: Life Insurance Carried

Name of Company	Face Amount	Cash Surrender Value	Loans	Beneficiary
TOTAL				

I/we authorize the Bank to make whatever credit inquiries it deems necessary in connection with this financial statement. I/we authorize and instruct any person or consumer reporting agency to furnish to the Bank any information that it may have or obtain in response to such credit inquiries.

I/we also hereby certify that no payment requirements listed herein are delinquent or in default except as follows; if "NONE" so state.

I/we fully understand that it is a federal crime punishable by fine or imprisonment or both to knowingly make any false statements concerning any of the above facts, pursuant to 18 U.S.C. Section 1014.

Applicant's		Date	Social	Date of
Signature _____		Signed	Security No.	Birth
		_____	_____	_____

Spouse's or				
Co-Applicant's		Date	Social	Date of
Signature _____		Signed	Security No.	Birth
		_____	_____	_____

STEP V: PROJECTIONS

<u>Projections you prepare should be for 3 years of both Balance Sheets and Income Statements.</u>

It is important for you to develop financial projections for your business due to these reasons:

- ✓ If you are a *start-up business*, developing the projections requires you to do initial, hopefully "eye opening" fact-finding research and then develop a list of assumptions under which you will base your projections. All of this when put together will provide your best "GUESSTIMATE" of your starting point and move on from there.

- ✓ If you are a *continuing business*, developing the projections requires you to study your past financial picture, hopefully in collaboration with your accountant. Realize any shortcomings and deal with them to move on to your next level of profitability with or without future expansions.

Either way, your projections will be looked at later by you and any financing source and for sure the financing source will pull these projections back out of the file later on when you begin providing them with the required actual interim and year end numbers. They will compare your projections with your actual numbers and see how well you are hitting your "mark". If the real performance differs a great deal from what was projected, be prepared for a discussion on why you missed your target(s), especially if you projected profitability and are showing a loss. You should be able to explain how you will adjust the projections going forward and how you intend on moving toward a brighter picture.

Whether you are a start-up or an existing business, your *research* used to develop your projections *should begin with information you gained from preparation of your* **Business Plan**. Your projections will be partially based upon:

> ➤ The size of your anticipated market of clients/customers
> ➤ The amount you have decided to charge for your products/services based upon the known researched competition
> ➤ Market cost of hiring and keeping the necessary qualified employees
> ➤ The amount of money you estimated would be needed just to open your doors or continue to keep the doors open
> ➤ The researched knowledge of various operating expenses such as space rent / space purchase; insurances; licensing; utilities estimate; transportation costs; shipping costs; accounting and legal; loan costs and repayment; bank fees; salary to self to cover your living expenses; office supplies; taxes; and a budget for blitz marketing.

The next important source of information to aid you in your projections should come from actual **Industry Standards.** Industry standards are developed by obtaining actual operating numbers from various businesses of varying sizes in varying industries classified by a *"NAICS" code number.* **NAICS** stands for <u>The North American Industry Classification System</u> which replaced the old SIC (Standard Industrial Classification) system. It is the standard used by Federal statistical agencies in classifying businesses for the purpose of collecting and analyzing business data. You may locate your NAICS number by using the web site: www.census.gov/eos/www/naics/

Two (2) known reliable sources for obtaining industry standards are:

1. "RMA"- Risk Management Association.
   Most banks subscribe to this service for doing comparisons of their customer's operational numbers to national industry standards. You may ask your bank's commercial loan department if they would provide you with the standards related to your industry and business size so that you might provide them with better projections when applying for your loan through them.
   The subscription cost is prohibitive for any one small business since you would not have need for continual use for the volumes of information provided.

2. "sageworks" Industry Data ("ProfitCents").

   "ProfitCents" is a group of web-based financial analysis tools used by many accountants and business consultants who often use the tools to win new clients or to begin new opportunities with existing clients.

   Ask your accountant if he or she would pull up the "ProfitCents" industry standards for your use for your particular size of business endeavor to aid you in completing financial projections. Of course you would assure them of your loyalty to use their services going forward. Again, the subscription cost is prohibitive for any one small business user.

How Industry Standards Aid in Financial Projections

Industry data obtained by such agencies as "RMA" and "sageworks" is not a "ball park" resolution to creation of your operating projections but should be used as a "benchmark" to assist you in your initial *guesstimates*. The data is gathered from all over the nation and is classified by NAICS code and by size of business as related to their annual revenues rather than by their exact ranking in that overall market.

From this data, you will find useful the following performance indicators which you may plug in to your guesstimates to give your projections more validity:

Income statement entries such as:

> Cost of Goods Sold as a % of revenues (sales)
> Gross profit margin as a % of revenues
> G & A expenses as a % of revenues
> Varying expense categories as a % of revenues such as the major categories of payroll, rent, and advertising
> EBITDA as a % of revenues
> Net income as a % of revenues

Balance sheet entries such as:

> Cash (bank funds) as a % of assets
> A/R as a % of assets
> Inventory as a % of assets
> Net fixed assets as a % of total assets
> Current liabilities, as compared to Assets
> Total liabilities, as compared to Assets

NOTE:

As a <u>new business</u>, you are working with your best guess estimates on revenue creation, growth percentages, and fairly well researched operating expense. If after plugging in industry standards, an entry doesn't make sense (+ or -) adjust it to the point it makes sense as again it is a best guess. However, it is better to be on the conservative side if you have to choose.

As an <u>existing business</u>, once you plug in the industry standards and compare the results with your past actual numbers you can see where you might be falling short or are ahead of the curve. Or, the projections may not feel realistic for your operations, so, adjust them to your comfort zone and what you are willing to commit to. Again, stay conservative.

Break even analysis

One final element in the creation of projections is a *Break Even Analysis.* This is an analysis to determine the point when revenues equal the costs (fixed and variable) associated with receiving the revenues.

Fixed costs are those that do not vary with sales volume such as rent and administrative salaries.

Variable costs are those that fluctuate directly with sales volume such as inventory purchases, shipping charges, and manufacturing costs.

The **SBA** (U.S. Small Business Administration) offers up the following formula:

"Breakeven point = fixed costs / (unit selling price – variable costs)"

The following is a sample of a breakeven analysis form:

Projected Revenues
_____

Fixed Costs:
_____
Salary Expense
Rent
Payroll taxes
Travel & Enter.
Prof. & Acctg
Depreciation
Insurance
Interest
Rep & Maint.
Util. & Phone
Office Supplies
Taxes
Other Expense

_____
Total Fixed Costs
_____

   (1) Cost of Goods Sold
        Percentage
_____

   (2) Breakeven Sales Level
_____

(1)   Total CGS (projected or actual) **divided by** Gross Sales or revenues
(2)   Total Fixed Costs **plus** [Projected Revenues **times** CGS percentage]

EXAMPLE: With projected revenues of $100,000 and a CGS % of 20% (or $20,000), and fixed costs of 50% (or $50,000), the breakeven sales level would be $70,000. Any sales amount below $70,000 would produce a loss and any sales amount over $70,000 would produce profit.

STEP VI: BANK RELATIONS / BANK LOANS

Banks still play an important part in business financing. After all, a big portion of the income for banks revolves around loan interest and loan fees.

Your first choice for a bank should be the bank you currently have your deposit relationship with. A bank is more likely to work with you if you have already established some sort of relationship with them.

When first approaching a bank for financing you need to be organized by having your detailed and previously reviewed loan request package ready. As discussed prior, this package should include:

Business Plan; Projections; Balance Sheets and P&Ls; Cash Flow; Tax Returns; Personal Financial Statement; Breakeven Analysis; A/R aging; A/P aging; and Report of Debts; Personal Resume; a copy of your organizational documents.

When looking at your request, the bank will measure you and your business by certain standards ("the C's of Credit"), namely:

➢ **Character**: Your experience and references. The way you treat your employees and customers. The way you take responsibility and fulfill your obligations.

➢ **Capacity**: Your track record of repayment. How much debt can your company handle? Ability to repay the debt. Remember: "cash flow is king".

➢ **Capital**: Your investment in your business. How liquid are your assets.

- ➤ **Conditions**: What are the current economic conditions? Is your company set up to handle the conditions? Can you weather any storm?
- ➤ **Collateral**: These are assets pledged to the loan. This is a part of the secondary source for repayment if cash flow fails. The bank will determine its value for lending purposes. Your personal guarantee will be a part of your collateral.

You should also be aware of your **personal credit** rating prior to approaching the bank. You have the ability to view your credit *report* once annually by going to www.annualcreditreport.com and obtain your published credit *score* at www.creditkarma.com. Keep in mind that any errors you believe are on the report must be formally disputed by you in writing. This process takes 30 to 45 days to get any corrections due you.

Personal Guarantees:

The bank will ask you and any person who owns 20% or more of your business to personally guarantee the loan. These guarantees may be either secured or unsecured. In the event the business is unable to repay the debt, your personal guarantee will require you to step in and personally begin repaying the debt (also, based upon any special negotiations you have arranged with the bank, if any, for this repayment).

Typical credit terms by Banks:

The Lender will want to test your commitment to your business by requesting that you have at least 20% "skin in the game" and therefore will rarely lend over 80% against the value of any collateral or cost of a project.

Loan types

Term Loan:

- Monthly Principal and interest payments
- Fixed and variable (floating) rates. If a floating rate, the payments may be based upon principal <u>plus</u> interest instead of principal <u>including</u> interest
- Used for asset acquisitions and term capital

Revolving Line of Credit:

- Typically monthly payments of interest only and principal due on pre-specified dates/intervals
- Typically, the term is for one year with the balance due in 12 months
- Used for short term working capital as in the need for carrying inventory and trade accounts receivable
- As the principal is paid down, the borrower may "come back to the well" and draw more funds up to the limit of the line

Non-Revolving Line of Credit (Draw Loan):

- Each draw carries pre-defined conditions
- Typically found in loans used for construction
- Once the limit of the loan has been drawn up there is no going "back to the well" as principal is reduced
- Typically converted to a term repayment at its maturity

Collateral Types (typical repayment term and % of financing):

Owner-occupied real estate:

- Up to 25 years
- 70% to 80% of value

Vacant real estate (land):

- Up to 5 years
- 65% of value

Equipment:

- 5 to 7 years
- 65% to 75% of value

Trade Accounts Receivable: *

- One year
- 50% to 75% of the value of receivables under 60 days past due
- The bank has the ability to disallow some receivables from the acceptable collateral
- Banks often use a "lock box" arrangement on these lines. The bank will set up a post office box under their control and you will invoice your receivable clients using the P.O. Box address as the place to remit their payments. The Bank will provide the Borrower with a list of who paid and in what amount and they will pay to principal, the amount borrowed against that receivable, and give the balance to the Borrower. That way the line continues to revolve up and down.

Inventory: *

- Up to 50% of the value of "finished goods" inventory
- Raw materials are typically not allowed

* Borrower will be required to submit a "Borrowing Base Report" to the bank monthly. The format is provided by the bank. It will verify the values of the A/R and Inventory on hand and assure that the borrowing guidelines are being adhered to.

Financial Ratios typically scrutinized by Banks:

1. *Debt Coverage Ratio* (cash to cover debt payments):
   Usually a 1.25x coverage is required (global cash flow available to cover global debt service)

2. *Debt-to-Equity Ratio*:
   Total Liabilities divided by Shareholder's Equity

3. *Current Ratio*:
   A liquidity ratio that estimates the ability of the Borrower to pay back short-term obligations. Current Assets / Current Liabilities

4. *Quick Ratio*:
   Shows the short term liquidity of the company. Compares short term debts with the most liquid assets. (Current Assets minus Inventories) / Current Liabilities

5. *Net Profit Margin*:
   Shows the efficiency of a company in cost control. The higher the net profit margin, the better a company is at converting its revenues into actual profit. Usually used to compare one company against another in the same industry. Net Profit / Net Sales

WHAT IF MY LOAN REQUEST IS TURNED DOWN????

- ✓ Get specific reasons for the decline
- ✓ The problem may be correctable
- ✓ Don't stop there. Try elsewhere. Why???
    1. Each financial institution has their own philosophies
    2. Lenders are only human. They too can have a bad day.
    3. You have the ability to correct any shortcomings.

MOVE ON!!!!

STEP VII: (marketing)

There have been and there continue to be volumes of very accessible work written about marketing strategy therefore I will not attempt to cover this subject with any detail or depth.

I can tell you that the wisdom and research offered on marketing can be found in many places including the public library and of course the internet.

<u>Things to be considered when developing a marketing plan</u>:

- A marketing plan is a necessity for **every** business and especially crucial for moving a start-up business forward. It's your *roadmap*.
- Even "word of mouth" advertising is a form of marketing strategy and the strategy enters when you strive to provide exemplary service to your clients/customers *all of the time* that will make them want to tell others about their wonderful experience and thus bring them in. Training your employees, who have direct contact with clients/customers, in the art of excellent service should be an ongoing event in the business. Don't let up or all will become lackadaisical and you lose.
- Calculate how much you are able to set aside out of your budget to spend on marketing. Then match that amount to types of marketing strategies available to you so that you can get the "biggest bang for your buck".
- Know who it is you are trying to reach. Who is your target market as described in your Business Plan? Which marketing strategies that you have researched will allow you to most effectively reach them?
- In your marketing strategy, "sell" what makes your business stand out. Sell your **uniqueness**. Perhaps getting your key employees involved in the brainstorming process to determine what your

business uniqueness is will strengthen the bond between all of you because they will be able to see what a key role they play in the business and its success. Hopefully, they are a key element of that uniqueness.

➢ Timing: What is your strong season? Market way ahead of this season and do follow-up.

➢ Finally, realize that marketing is a numbers game. Out of the many contacts you reach, only a small percentage will respond in your favor. Therefore, utilize more than one strategy and reach as many in your target market as you possibly can.

A Few Marketing Resources:

❖ Linkedin:
Get your name out there along with your business and its uniqueness. Stay active.

❖ Public Library membership:
Each library has online resources for your use. Their databases provide information on business insights. Also see: "Reference USA".

❖ MailChimp.com: Free email blast campaigns to reach up to 2,000 people by email for advertising/marketing.

STEP VIII: RESOURCES

Where do I find assistance for my business endeavors at my price??

SBDC: THE SMALL BUSINESS DEVELOPMENT CENTERS

Find them at: www.americassbdc.org

This organization is partially funded by the U.S. Small Business Administration (SBA) and state and local governments, as well as private sector resources. According to the SBA there are "63 Host networks branching out with more than 900 service delivery points throughout the U.S. and its territories". These hosts include "48 university-sponsored SBDC hosts; 8 Community college-sponsored SBDC hosts; and 7 State-sponsored Lead SBDCs".

The SBDC provides technical assistance to small businesses and entrepreneurs. They support business growth and strength and hence they create local and regional economic impact through capital formation; revenues growth; and job creation and retention.

The services provided are free and they are delivered by business counselors/analysts who have true life and business experiences through their own business ownership; careers in the finance industry; business leadership; and educational backgrounds. Some of the assistance categories are business plan development; financial planning/analysis; marketing; and social media.

The SBDC is also known for their free courses/workshops for entrepreneurs and entrepreneurial hopefuls.

The U.S. Small Business Administration (SBA):

Find them at: www.sba.gov

Found in most major U.S. cities, the SBA works with local lenders to provide them with an incentive to make loans to small businesses including start-ups. This incentive comes in the form of providing the lender with a partial loan guarantee that can be as high as 75% to 90% of the loan. SBA loans benefit the small business borrower by allowing the borrower to find loan repayment plans that have a longer repayment term than normal with competitive loan rates and somewhat relaxed loan qualifiers.

Contact your local office and obtain a list of participating lenders in your community and attend some of the SBA community events that explain the various types of bank loans guaranteed by the SBA. The SBA also offers many in-person and online training courses and videos. Topics covered include: (this is just a sampling of what is offered)

Government contracting
Customer service
Financing the business
Hiring employees
Intellectual property
HUB Zone operation
Crowdfunding
Pre-8(a) contractor training
Women Owned Small Business (WOSB) programs
Business Plans
Marketing
Franchising

ACCION:

Find them at: www.us.accion.org

The ACCION U.S. network is the largest nationwide micro and small business lending network in the United States. There are at least 25 field offices.

ACCION makes it possible for small businesses (many with five or fewer employees) to gain access to the financial services they need to expand. By the way, these small businesses make up about 85% of all businesses in the United States and many are too small to obtain financing from the normal providers. They are known to provide loans from as small as $200 up to a maximum today of over $300,000.

SCORE (Service Corps of Retired Executives):

Directly supported by the SBA. These are volunteers from the community who offer their time and past business experience in service to small business entrepreneurs and entrepreneur hopefuls. A good source of one-on-one business counseling.

Universities and Community Colleges:

Many locations have business incubators for business start-ups as well as actual curriculum geared toward entrepreneurism.

Chambers of Commerce:

Most have programs for small business education and all schedule several good networking events throughout the year during which you will have time to visit with other businesses and network your business. They also promote minority business ownership.

<u>www.life-global.org</u> (HP Life-e-Learning):

Direct quote from the web site: "HP Learning Initiative for Entrepreneurs (HP LIFE) is a global program that trains students, entrepreneurs, and small business owners like you to apply IT and business skills, so you can establish and grow a business, build successful companies and create jobs. Our face-to-face trainings, tools and e-Learning program address educational needs, improve and strengthen skills and enable you to move forward".

Their online training programs are **_free_** and they are interactive, self-paced and full of practical experiences.

<u>www.xero.com</u>:

This is a small business software site that is affordable ($9; $30; or $70 per month). This software I have been told allows the subscriber to see cash flow in real time; do bank reconciliations by importing and coding bank transactions; invoicing customers by creating those invoices and sending them; getting paid online; and lots of other add-ons. I believe the $9 per month variety is just right for many start-up small businesses and the $30/month variety is called the "standard" plan.

www.ingramcontent.com/pod-product-compliance
Lightning Source LLC
Chambersburg PA
CBHW081233020426
42331CB00012B/3161